LIVING YOUR LOVE STORY OFFICIAL WORKBOOK

TIMELESS WISDOM FOR DATING, MARRIAGE, AND INTIMACY

PHIL HOPPER

D DESTINY IMAGE

Copyright 2024–Destiny Image

All rights reserved. This book is protected by the copyright laws of the United States of America. This book may not be copied or reprinted for commercial gain or profit. The use of short quotations or occasional page copying for personal or group study is permitted and encouraged. Permission will be granted upon request. Unless otherwise indicated, all scripture quotations are taken from the *King James Version* of the Bible. Used by permission. All rights reserved.

All emphasis within Scripture quotations is the author's own. Please note that Destiny Image's publishing style capitalizes certain pronouns in Scripture that refer to the Father, Son, and Holy Spirit, and may differ from some publishers' styles. Take note that the name satan and related names are not capitalized. We choose not to acknowledge him, even to the point of violating grammatical rules.

Destiny Image P.O. Box 310, Shippensburg, PA 17257-0310

This book and all other Destiny Image's books are available at Christian bookstores and distributors worldwide.

For Worldwide Distribution, Printed in the U.S.A.

Reach us on the Internet: www.destinyimage.com.

ISBN 13 TP: 9798881504441

ISBN 13 eBook: 9798881504458

CONTENTS

Introduction v
1. It's Time to Define the Relationship 1
2. The Betrothal 8
3. Single, Satisfied, and Ready 14
4. Patient and Passionate 20
5. More than a Feeling 26
6. His Needs; Her Needs 31
7. More than Meets the Eye 36
8. Sacred and Sizzling Sex 43
9. When You've Lost That Lovin' Feelin' 50
10. How to Get Back that Lovin' Feelin' 57
11. The Gardener 64
12. Loving Your Second Like Your First 70

About the Publisher 77

INTRODUCTION

Welcome to the "Living Your Love Story Official Workbook," an enriching journey designed to deepen your understanding and appreciation of the love shared with your partner. This workbook serves as your guide through the profound wisdom embedded within the Song of Solomon, an exploration of love, commitment, and intimacy that transcends time. As you navigate through each chapter of this workbook, you'll encounter structured insights, practical exercises, and reflective questions tailored to help you cultivate a stronger, more fulfilling relationship with your spouse.

WHAT YOU CAN EXPECT FROM THIS WORKBOOK

- **A Deeper Understanding of Love's Evolution**: Love is not static; it evolves, matures, and deepens. Throughout this workbook, you'll explore the different stages of a relationship—from the first flush of love in the early days to the rich, deep connection that develops over decades. Each section of this workbook draws on key moments from the Song of Solomon to illustrate these stages, providing both scriptural insights and real-life applications.

- **Practical Tools for Nurturing Your Relationship**: The workbook offers practical exercises that prompt both reflection and action. These include journaling prompts, discussion questions for you and your partner, and actionable steps to implement the principles discussed. By engaging with these tools, you and your partner can develop new ways to communicate, express affection, and support each other through life's challenges.

- **Insights into the Spiritual Dimensions of Love**: Recognizing that love is both an emotional and spiritual journey, this workbook delves into how your relationship can reflect and enhance your spiritual beliefs. You will explore how principles such as forgiveness, patience, and selflessness play out in a loving partnership and how they can lead to a more harmonious and spiritually aligned life.

- **Strategies for Overcoming Common Marital Challenges**: No relationship is without its hurdles. This workbook addresses common challenges such as communication breakdowns, differing expectations, and external pressures, providing biblical wisdom and modern strategies for navigating these issues. You will learn how to fortify your relationship against potential pitfalls and how to repair it when things go awry.

- **Renewed Appreciation for Your Partner**: As you progress through the workbook, you'll be encouraged to view your partner in new light. By revisiting the

INTRODUCTION

reasons you fell in love, assessing the growth you've experienced together, and celebrating your journey, you'll renew your appreciation for your partner and the unique qualities they bring to your life.

HOW TO USE THIS WORKBOOK

This workbook is designed to be flexible, allowing you to work through the chapters at your own pace, either individually or as a couple. Each chapter contains the following elements:

- **10 Key Points Summary**: These summaries distill the essence of each chapter, highlighting major themes and takeaways that are crucial for understanding and applying the lessons of Song of Solomon to your own relationship.
- **Reflective Questions**: These questions are designed to provoke thought and discussion, helping you to consider how the concepts discussed might be relevant to your own life and relationship. They can be used as conversation starters or as journal prompts for deeper introspection.
- **Actionable Steps**: Each chapter includes three actionable steps—Cultivate, Equip, and Engage. These steps are designed to move you from reflection to action, providing clear tasks that help you to apply the lessons of the workbook to your daily life and relationship.
- **Word of Encouragement**: This section provides a short, uplifting message to inspire you and reinforce the spiritual dimensions of the lessons learned.
- **Bible Verse**: Each encouragement is paired with a relevant Bible verse from the New King James

INTRODUCTION

Version, grounding the workbook's teachings in scriptural authority.
- **Journaling Prompt**: To deepen your engagement with the material, each chapter concludes with a prompt for journaling. This exercise encourages personal reflection and helps solidify the lessons learned.

"Living Your Love Story Official Workbook" is more than just a tool for improving relationships—it's a pathway to discovering the richness of life shared with another, grounded in love and guided by faith. Whether you are newly in love or seeking to rekindle the flames of a long-standing relationship, this workbook offers valuable insights and practical advice for nurturing your partnership in meaningful ways. Welcome to a transformative experience that will not only deepen your understanding of what it means to love but also enrich your journey together.

CHAPTER 1
IT'S TIME TO DEFINE THE RELATIONSHIP

In the journey of defining relationships and understanding love, remember that Christ's pursuit of us is the greatest example of love. He invites us to respond to His love and commit fully to Him.

"Greater love has no one than this, than to lay down one's life for his friends." - John 15:13 (NKJV)

In this chapter, I explore the intertwining paths of personal risk and divine providence in shaping our most crucial relationships. **Defining Love and Risk**, I share a pivotal moment from my college days at the University of Kansas, where I juggled a promising football career with a burgeoning romance. Despite strict team rules prohibiting romantic distractions, the unexpected visit from Christa, the girl with green eyes, tempted me to risk everything. This personal anecdote is not just about youthful rebellion but underscores a deeper narrative about the risks we take for love and the rewards they can sometimes bring.

As I reflect on these events, I recognize that it wasn't mere chance that allowed my relationship with Christa to flourish without repercussion. **The Intervention of Providence** seemed to play a hand in shielding us from potential consequences. This notion of providence resonates deeply with the biblical story of Solomon, a figure whose life and decisions often mirrored the balance between divine fate and personal choice. Through this lens, we can see how our own lives might also be part of a greater plan, guided by a hand that weaves our stories into the larger tapestry of life.

In drawing parallels between biblical narratives and personal experiences, I delve into how Solomon represents **The Biblical Parallel of Solomon and Jesus**. Both figures, heralded as shepherds and kings, exemplify leadership that is compassionate yet authoritative. Solomon's role as a shepherd king in the Song of Solomon beautifully prefigures Christ's pastoral care and kingly sovereignty in the New Testament. This duality enriches our understanding of how leadership and love can be exercised in both gentle guidance and sovereign rule.

Cultural perceptions deeply influence how we see ourselves and others. In the story of the Shulamite, we confront **Cultural Perceptions of Beauty**. Her dark skin, a result of laboring in the vineyards, becomes a source of shame due to cultural standards that favored paler complexions. This historical context invites us to question our own cultural biases and consider how they shape our perceptions of beauty and worth. It's a compelling reminder that what is deemed beautiful in one culture may be seen differently in another, urging a more inclusive understanding of beauty.

The allegory of Solomon and the Shulamite extends beyond a mere love story, serving as a profound **Spiritual Allegory of Love and Redemption**. Their narrative mirrors Christ's relationship with the Church—His bride, whom He redeems and sanctifies. This spiritual romance emphasizes that true love is redemptive and transformative, capable of transcending our past and imperfections. It's a powerful metaphor for the unconditional love Christ offers to us, his followers.

The ancient tradition of verifying a bride's purity through a blood-stained cloth on the wedding night illustrates the **Importance of Sexual Purity**. This practice, deeply embedded in cultural and religious traditions, symbolizes the high value placed on moral integrity and purity. Reflecting on this, we gain insights into the pressures and expectations placed on individuals within their cultural contexts and are reminded of the continuing importance of integrity in our personal lives.

In the deeply **The Unforgiving Nature of Honor-Based Cultures**, the Shulamite woman's experience is a stark illustration of the consequences of societal shame and familial dishonor. Her story encourages us to consider the harsh realities faced by those who transgress societal norms and the grace needed to restore those who have fallen into disgrace. It prompts us to extend forgiveness and support to those around us who struggle under the weight of cultural condemnation.

Today's dating culture often features ambiguous terms and fluid dynamics, which I address in discussing **Modern Relationship Dynamics**. Young adults frequently navigate a complex web of relationships, where clear definitions are eschewed in favor of more casual connections. This shifting landscape calls for a return to clarity and intentionality in relationships, principles that are foundational to both healthy interpersonal relationships and a robust faith life.

Jesus' Pursuit of the Believer is a theme that resonates throughout scripture and life. Just as I pursued Christa, not willing to give up despite obstacles, Jesus pursues us with relentless love. However, there comes a time when continued rejection can lead to a withdrawal of this pursuit. This narrative serves as a stark reminder of the seriousness with which we should approach our relationship with Christ, acknowledging His sacrifice and responding with committed love.

Finally, the ultimate **The Eternal Love Story** is found in the union of Christ and His Church, a theme that runs from Genesis to Revelation. The biblical narrative culminates in the marriage supper of the Lamb, where Christ, the bridegroom, is united forever with His bride. This eternal love story is the greatest ever told, offering us hope and a future with Him at the end of the age.

Through these reflections, my aim is to guide you into a deeper understanding of how these themes not only apply to biblical figures or past cultures but are relevant to our lives today. By examining our relationships through the lens of scripture, we gain invaluable insights into love, redemption, and divine purpose.

REFLECTIVE QUESTIONS

1. **Personal Risk for Love:** How have you personally risked for love, and what did those choices teach you about your priorities and values?
2. **Divine Providence in Relationships:** Can you identify moments in your relationships that felt guided by providence or fate? How did those moments shape your relationship's trajectory?
3. **Cultural Standards of Beauty:** How do societal standards of beauty influence your self-perception and interactions with others? Are there areas where you need to embrace a more grace-filled view of beauty?
4. **Spiritual Redemption:** Reflect on a time when you experienced redemption, either spiritually or

emotionally. How did this change your understanding of forgiveness and grace?
5. **Defining Modern Relationships**: In today's culture, what challenges do you face in defining relationships clearly? How can you apply biblical principles to guide these relationships?

Actionable Steps

- **Cultivate a Deeper Understanding of Love**: Spend time meditating on 1 Corinthians 13 and reflect on how you can embody this biblical definition of love in your personal relationships.
- **Equip Yourself with Wisdom in Relationships**: Engage in a Bible study focusing on the lives of Solomon and Jesus to understand how their leadership and sacrificial love can inform your relationship dynamics.
- **Engage Others in Conversations About Cultural Perceptions**: Initiate discussions with friends or a community group about how cultural perceptions of beauty and honor influence our relationships and self-esteem.

Journaling Prompt

Reflect on the relationship between Solomon and the Shulamite as a metaphor for Christ and the Church. How does understanding this relationship change your view of God's love for you and your response to Him?

IT'S TIME TO DEFINE THE RELATIONSHIP

LIVING YOUR LOVE STORY OFFICIAL WORKBOOK

CHAPTER 2
THE BETROTHAL

Reflecting on the beautiful process of betrothal and marriage as it was traditionally practiced by the ancient Hebrews reminds us of the sacred commitment that defines our relationship with our Bridegroom, the Lord Jesus Christ. As He has promised to return for us, preparing a place in His Father's house, so we must prepare ourselves, maintaining purity and readiness for His return.

"In My Father's house are many mansions; if it were not so, I would have told you. I go to prepare a place for you. And if I go and prepare a place for you, I will come again and receive you to Myself; that where I am, there you may be also" - John 14:2-3 (NKJV)

Reflecting on my son Jake's thoughtful proposal planning brings to mind the elaborate and deeply symbolic **ancient proposal ceremony of the Jewish bridegroom and bride**. This tradition beautifully illustrates our relationship with Christ. The betrothal stage, marked by the signing of the Ketubah, was not just an engagement but a binding contract that set the terms of marriage, emphasizing the seriousness and commitment that should also characterize our relationship with Jesus. This covenant was as binding as marriage itself, requiring faithfulness even before the couple lived together or consummated their union, highlighting the depth of commitment expected in our relationship with Christ.

The process of the bridegroom preparing a place for his bride resonates deeply with **Jesus's promise to prepare a place for us** in His Father's house. This act of preparation is a profound expression of care and anticipation, mirroring the preparations we should make in our hearts and lives as we await His return. It is a reminder of the intentional and purposeful work Jesus is doing on our behalf, which should inspire us to live lives that are pleasing to Him.

The consummation and celebration of the marriage, which included a seven-day feast, underscores the **joy and sanctity of the wedding.** Just as the ancient weddings were a community celebration, our eventual reunion with Christ will be a joyous, communal celebration in heaven. This stage of the wedding not only emphasized the physical union of the bride and groom but also celebrated the spiritual and communal aspects of marriage, reflecting how our union with Christ will be both personal and part of a larger heavenly community.

Today Could Be "The Day" is a recurring theme throughout the chapter, emphasizing the need for constant readiness. The ancient Jewish bride lived in a state of preparedness, knowing that her bridegroom could return at any moment. This mirrors how we, as believers, should live in anticipation of Christ's return, keeping ourselves pure and devoted, fully committed to our faith without distraction.

The chapter also delves into the painful reality of spiritual adultery through **sinning and cheating on Jesus, our Bride-**

groom. Just as a faithful spouse would not entertain thoughts of infidelity, we are called to remain spiritually faithful to Jesus. Sin is portrayed not just as a moral failing, but as a betrayal of our relationship with Christ, akin to spiritual adultery. This stark analogy serves to heighten our awareness of sin's seriousness and its impact on our relationship with God.

Reflective Questions

1. **Understanding of Ancient Traditions:** How does understanding the ancient Jewish betrothal process deepen your appreciation for the relationship between Christ and the Church?
2. **Readiness for Christ's Return:** In what ways are you preparing your heart and life for Jesus' return, and how can you improve in this area?
3. **Joy and Celebration of Union:** How does the concept of the wedding feast relate to your understanding of heaven and the communal aspect of our future with Christ?
4. **Constant Readiness:** Reflect on how living in anticipation of Christ's return affects your daily decisions and spiritual discipline.
5. **Faithfulness to Our Commitments:** How does the metaphor of marital faithfulness help you understand your relationship with Jesus and the seriousness of sin?

Actionable Steps

- **Cultivate Readiness and Purity:** Regularly examine your life and heart to ensure they align with God's will, as a bride prepares for her wedding day.
- **Equip Yourself with Knowledge of Biblical Prophecy:** Study the prophetic scriptures that describe Jesus' return to deepen your understanding and anticipation of that glorious day.
- **Engage in Community with Believers:** Strengthen bonds with your church and community to foster a supportive environment that encourages spiritual readiness and growth.

Journaling Prompt

Reflect on the parallels between the ancient Jewish wedding practices and our relationship with Christ. Consider how this perspective influences your view of commitment, readiness, and faithfulness in your spiritual life.

THE BETROTHAL

LIVING YOUR LOVE STORY OFFICIAL WORKBOOK

CHAPTER 3
SINGLE, SATISFIED, AND READY

In a world that often equates happiness with relationships, it is crucial to find your true satisfaction in your relationship with Jesus. Being single is not a transitional phase but a significant season that holds profound potential for personal and spiritual growth. Recognizing that Christ alone has the power to complete you is foundational to experiencing true contentment, whether single or married.

"But I want you to be without care. He who is unmarried cares for the things of the Lord—how he may please the Lord. But he who is married cares about the things of the world—how he may please his wife." - 1 Corinthians 7:32-34 (NKJV)

The beginning of Song of Solomon, when Solomon and the young maiden are single, sets the perfect backdrop for discussing **contentment in singleness**. It's a myth that marriage is a cure-all for discontent. True contentment is found in Christ alone because no human relationship can fulfill the deepest needs of your heart like Jesus can. Understanding this can transform how you view your single years, not as a waiting period but as a time of valuable and fulfilling relationship with Christ.

The discussion of **the ancient Jewish betrothal process** provides a poignant reminder of the seriousness with which commitments were made, reflecting the gravity with which we should approach our relationship with Christ. In modern terms, while the engagement might seem less formal, the spiritual implication of being betrothed to Christ involves a profound dedication and preparation for eternal union.

The theme **"Today Could Be 'The Day'"** captures the essence of living in a state of readiness. Just as the Jewish bride lived in anticipation of her bridegroom's return, so should we live in constant readiness for Jesus' return, striving to maintain purity and devotion amidst a world of distractions.

Discussing **contentment versus expectations** highlights a common pitfall among both singles and married individuals—the expectation that another person will complete them. This section is critical as it underscores the importance of finding completion and satisfaction in Christ alone, preventing unrealistic expectations that can lead to disappointment in relationships.

The reality of sin as spiritual adultery is a powerful analogy used to describe how deviating from our faithfulness to Christ can be likened to cheating in a marriage. This analogy serves to heighten awareness of the seriousness of sin and the fidelity we owe to our spiritual relationship with Jesus.

Reflective Questions

1. **Contentment in Singleness:** How does your relationship with Christ influence your contentment in your current life stage?
2. **Preparation for Christ's Return:** In what practical ways can you prepare yourself daily for the return of Christ, similar to how the Jewish bride prepared for her bridegroom?
3. **Expectations of Marriage:** How have your expectations of marriage been shaped by your relationship with Christ?
4. **Readiness and Anticipation:** How does living in anticipation of Christ's return influence your actions and decisions today?
5. **Spiritual Fidelity:** What does spiritual fidelity mean to you, and how do you practice it in your daily life?

Actionable Steps

- **Cultivate a Relationship with Christ:** Spend time daily in prayer and Bible study to deepen your relationship with Christ, ensuring that He is the foundation of your contentment.
- **Equip Yourself with Patience and Understanding:** Learn more about biblical teachings on marriage and singleness to equip yourself with a godly perspective that enhances your understanding and patience.
- **Engage in Meaningful Community:** Participate actively in a church or community group that supports your spiritual growth and helps you

maintain a focus on living for Christ in anticipation of His return.

Journaling **Prompt**

Reflect on how the concept of being "single, satisfied, and ready" challenges or affirms your current views on singleness and contentment. How can you apply this understanding to enhance your relationship with Christ and others?

LIVING YOUR LOVE STORY OFFICIAL WORKBOOK

CHAPTER 4

PATIENT AND PASSIONATE

In your journey through life and relationships, embrace patience and passion with grace. These virtues are not just ideals but practical approaches that enhance every aspect of our lives, reflecting our deepest faith in action. Remember, the most profound expressions of love come through patient devotion and passionate commitment, not just in moments of joy but also through challenges.

Ephesians 5:25 - "Husbands, love your wives, just as Christ also loved the church and gave Himself for her."

As we journey together through the profound relationship described in Ephesians 5:22-33, we discover that **Marriage as a Divine Metaphor** not only grounds us in our daily lives but elevates our understanding of spiritual truths. Marriage, my dear readers, is more than a human institution; it's a divine symbol of the union between Christ and His Church. This sacred metaphor teaches us that just as Christ loves the Church with patience and sacrifice, so too should husbands and wives commit to each other, mirroring this holy commitment.

In your own relationships, whether you are preparing for marriage or seeking to strengthen your bond, remember that **Sexual Purity and Holiness** are not outdated concepts but foundational to honoring God within the covenant of marriage. The Song of Solomon beautifully illustrates the passionate yet pure love between Solomon and his bride, emphasizing that true love waits for the right time. This waiting enriches the relationship, making the eventual union not only a fulfillment of desire but a consecration of love under God's gaze.

Furthermore, we learn that **God's Timing for Love** is perfect. It's a reminder to us all not to rush into love or awaken it before its time. There is wisdom in waiting, wisdom in preparing your heart and soul for the one you will love. By doing so, you align your most intimate human desires with the divine rhythm set by our Creator.

One of the most solemn aspects of marriage that we often overlook is that **Marriage is a Covenant**. This covenant is not merely a contract or an agreement; it is a sacred vow that echoes the promises God makes to His people. Just as God is faithful to His covenants, we too are called to maintain fidelity and steadfast love within the bounds of marriage.

The permanence of this bond is highlighted in **The Unbreakable Bond in Marriage**. Marriage was intended by God to be a lifelong commitment, where "a man shall leave his father and mother and be joined to his wife, and they shall become one flesh." This unity is not easily dissolved and should not be entered into lightly or without deep consideration and prayer.

REFLECTIVE QUESTIONS

1. How does viewing marriage as a reflection of Christ's relationship with the Church influence our approach to our own marriages?
2. Are we prepared to honor God in our relationships, maintaining purity and patience even in a world that often encourages the opposite?
3. Are we mindful of the sanctity of the marriage covenant, treating it not just as a legal formality but as a binding spiritual commitment?
4. How can we strengthen this unbreakable bond daily, choosing love, forgiveness, and patience, even when challenged?
5. As we engage with our communities, how can we support one another in our journeys toward or within marriage, providing wisdom, accountability, and encouragement?

ACTIONABLE STEPS

- **Cultivate**: Foster environments in your life where patience and passion for God's timing can flourish. This means embracing community and accountability with those who will encourage you to maintain your commitments.
- **Equip**: Arm yourself with knowledge of God's Word regarding relationships and marriage. Study Scriptures that detail the sanctity of the marriage covenant and the roles each partner should play.

- **Engage**: Actively participate in ministries or groups that support the value of biblical marriage. Whether single or married, contribute to discussions and activities that uphold the virtues of patience, purity, and lifelong commitment.

Journaling Prompt

Reflect on how the metaphor of marriage as described in Ephesians 5 can influence your current or future relationships. How does this perspective shape your understanding of love, sacrifice, and commitment in your daily life? Write about steps you might take to align more closely with this divine example.

PATIENT AND PASSIONATE

LIVING YOUR LOVE STORY OFFICIAL WORKBOOK

CHAPTER 5
MORE THAN A FEELING

Love is more than a feeling, it's a commitment and a decision. For those who are single or already in a relationship, understanding that love requires intentionality is crucial. It's easy to fall in love, but staying in love requires conscious effort and choice. This chapter guides you through the intentional steps of dating with the end goal of a sustainable, fulfilling marriage.

James 1:17 - "Every good gift and every perfect gift is from above, and comes down from the Father of lights, with whom there is no variation or shadow of turning."

In this journey of love and relationship, we find that **Dating Intentionally** sets the foundation. It's vital to date with the clear intention of discovering compatibility and building a relationship that leads to marriage. This means evaluating emotional and spiritual maturity, as well as readiness for commitment, which are essential for a healthy relationship that endures life's challenges.

Moreover, understanding that **Emotional and Spiritual Maturity** is fundamental can help prevent the pain of rushed emotional entanglements. This maturity allows you to enter a relationship with a whole and healthy heart, ensuring both individuals are prepared for the lifelong commitment that marriage requires.

As you navigate through dating, it's important to recognize that **Courtship Has a Purpose**. Moving from dating to courtship signifies a readiness to explore a deeper commitment and should be marked by mutual respect, shared values, and the clear intention toward marriage. Courtship is the time to deepen understanding of each other's character, values, and life visions.

Engagement and Preparation for Marriage follows courtship when both individuals are confident in their decision to commit for life. This stage involves practical preparations for marriage but should remain concise to maintain focus and prevent unnecessary temptations.

Lastly, entering into **Marriage as a Covenant** highlights that marriage, in God's design, is more than a legal contract; it is a lifelong covenant. This stage underscores the commitment to face life together, embracing all challenges and joys, under the covenant that mirrors Christ's commitment to His church.

Reflective Questions

1. How does understanding love as a choice change your approach to relationships?
2. What steps can you take to ensure you are emotionally and spiritually mature before entering a serious relationship?
3. In what ways can you practice intentionality during the dating phase?

4. How can the concept of courtship strengthen the foundation for a lasting marriage?
5. What does it mean to view marriage as a covenant rather than a contract?

Actionable Steps

- **Cultivate** personal growth by actively pursuing spiritual and emotional maturity before seeking a serious relationship.
- **Equip** yourself with knowledge about the biblical perspective on relationships and marriage to understand the significance of each stage in the relationship progression.
- **Engage** in communities or groups that support healthy relationship practices and provide accountability.

Journaling Prompt

Reflect on the current or desired stages of your relationship. How can you apply the principles of intentional dating, courtship, and preparation for marriage to cultivate a relationship that is not only lasting but also enriching and fulfilling? Write about the specific steps you can take to move towards these goals in your personal life.

LIVING YOUR LOVE STORY OFFICIAL WORKBOOK

MORE THAN A FEELING

CHAPTER 6
HIS NEEDS; HER NEEDS

Understanding the unique emotional needs of men and women is crucial for developing deep and lasting relationships. As we explore the dynamics between Solomon and the Shulamite in the Song of Solomon, we see a beautiful depiction of how recognizing and respecting each other's needs can lead to a profound emotional connection. This chapter delves into the essentials of fulfilling these needs within the sacred covenant of marriage.

Hebrews 13:4 - "Marriage is honorable among all, and the bed undefiled; but fornicators and adulterers God will judge."

In this journey of love and relationship, we start with the recognition that **Men and Women are Uniquely Created**. God made us male and female, each with distinct emotional landscapes. Understanding these differences is not about reinforcing stereotypes but about acknowledging how God uniquely designed our emotional needs.

Emotional Bank Accounts play a critical role in relationships. Every interaction either deposits or withdraws from our emotional reserves. Successful relationships focus on building these accounts with positive, affirming interactions, avoiding the overdrawn status that leads to conflicts and disconnection.

The concept of **Intimacy Beyond the Physical** reveals that true intimacy involves emotional, mental, and spiritual connections. Intimacy can be defined as 'into-me-see,' where partners share their deepest selves, which is foundational for a fulfilling sexual relationship within marriage.

Understanding and Meeting Emotional Needs is essential for marital happiness. For a woman, feeling cherished and celebrated for her beauty and for a man, being respected and admired for his strength are key. Each partner must strive to meet these core needs to maintain a healthy, vibrant relationship.

Finally, **Building and Maintaining Emotional Connections** in marriage requires intentional actions that affirm each other's core emotional needs. This ongoing effort helps to sustain love and passion over the long term, making each phase of marriage richer and more fulfilling.

REFLECTIVE QUESTIONS

1. How do you currently address the unique emotional needs of your partner?
2. In what ways can you improve your emotional deposits into your partner's life?
3. How can you foster deeper intimacy in your relationship beyond physical affection?
4. What steps can you take to better understand and meet your partner's deepest emotional needs?

5. How can your relationship benefit from a deeper understanding of the biblical perspective on emotional needs?

ACTIONABLE STEPS

- **Cultivate** deeper emotional connections by regularly discussing your feelings and needs openly and honestly with your partner.
- **Equip** yourself with knowledge of your partner's specific emotional needs and preferences by asking direct questions and observing their responses in different situations.
- **Engage** in regular, intentional acts that specifically meet your partner's emotional needs, such as planned date nights, thoughtful gifts, or words of affirmation.

JOURNALING Prompt

Reflect on your relationship's current emotional health. Are there areas where you feel more could be done to meet your emotional needs or those of your partner? Journal about specific actions you can take this week to make positive deposits into your partner's emotional bank account.

HIS NEEDS; HER NEEDS

LIVING YOUR LOVE STORY OFFICIAL WORKBOOK

CHAPTER 7
MORE THAN MEETS THE EYE

"Be steadfast, immovable, always abounding in the work of the Lord, knowing that in the Lord your labor is not in vain."
- 1 Corinthians 15:58, NKJV

"Let not your heart be troubled; you believe in God, believe also in Me. In My Father's house are many mansions; if it were not so, I would have told you. I go to prepare a place for you." - John 14:1-2, NKJV

In our journey through Song of Solomon, we encounter profound truths about the sacred institution of marriage, which is more than just a social contract; it's a divine metaphor for Christ's love for His Church. As we explore this narrative, we understand that **Symbolism of Marriage** is not merely about human companionship but a reflection of a heavenly promise. It portrays the covenant between Christ and His bride—the Church—with each ritual and symbol enriching our understanding of divine love.

In the ancient rituals of a Hebrew wedding, which are vividly depicted in our text, there is significant spiritual meaning. The process of setting a dowry and initiating the marriage covenant mirrors the redemptive act of Christ. Through this, we learn that the **Hebrew Wedding Rituals** are not archaic traditions but illustrations of the price Christ paid, showing the immense value He places on His relationship with us. This dowry, then, is akin to the sacrifice of Jesus on the cross, purchased not with perishable items but with His very life, which He laid down for His beloved.

At the Last Supper, Jesus established a new covenant with His disciples, akin to the marital covenants of old, where wine was shared as a symbol of agreement and mutual commitment. This act of communion is our modern connection to that sacred promise, reminding us that the **Covenant of Communion** at the Last Supper was Jesus' way of sealing His promises with His blood, foreshadowing His ultimate sacrifice for humanity's sins. Each time we partake in communion, we reaffirm our place in this eternal covenant, echoing the ancient betrothal tradition.

In the narrative of Solomon and his bride, we see an anticipatory joy as the groom prepares a place for his bride, reflecting Jesus' promise to prepare a place for us in His Father's house. This **Preparation and Anticipation** should fill us with hope as we live in the expectation of Christ's return, mirroring the bride's preparations for her new life with Solomon. This anticipation is not passive but active, as we ready ourselves spiritually and morally for the day we will be united with our Bridegroom.

Amidst this hopeful waiting, the Shulamite experiences profound anxiety and insecurity, fears that resonate with many of us as we navigate our spiritual journey. The recurring dreams of the bride in Song of Solomon reveal her deepest fears and insecurities, a reminder that like the Shulamite, we too might feel forgotten or overlooked. However, these **Anxiety and Insecurity in Waiting** teach us that our feelings do not dictate the faithfulness of our Bridegroom. They prompt us to trust not in our perception but in the promise of His Word.

One of the most transformative aspects of marriage, as depicted in Scripture, is its role in our sanctification. Marriage challenges us, refines us, and teaches us about unconditional love, much like Christ's love for the Church. Through this lens, we see that **Sanctification Through Marriage** is God's tool for refining us, helping us grow in grace, patience, and love—qualities that reflect Christ's character.

The Apostle Paul, in Ephesians 5, elaborates on the roles within a Christian marriage, which serve as a living metaphor for the relationship between Christ and the Church. The **Divine Design of Marital Roles** reveals that husbands and wives have specific, God-given roles that, when embraced in humility and love, display a picture of Christ's sacrificial love for us. Husbands are called to love as Christ loved the Church, and wives are invited to respond in supportive submission, mirroring the Church's respect for Christ.

As we delve deeper into the wedding customs of ancient Hebrew culture, the **Symbolism of the Bridal Chamber** stands out, representing the private and sacred union between Christ and His Church. This imagery is rich with anticipation for the church today, as it awaits the consummation of Christ's kingdom at His return. It is a profound reminder of the intimate and eternal fellowship we are promised with our Savior.

The narrative and customs we explore in Song of Solomon are not just historical or cultural relics but vibrant illustrations of the **Eternal Unity Promised** between Christ and His Church. Each element of the Hebrew wedding process—from the betrothal to the wedding feast—provides a deeper understanding of what it means to be united with Christ forever. This eternal perspective transforms how we live today, fostering a life of purity, readiness, and devotion.

Finally, as we consider Solomon's role as both shepherd and king, we are reminded that **Christ as the Ultimate Fulfillment** of all God's promises. The dual roles of Solomon foreshadow the first and second coming of Christ—first as a humble shepherd who lays down His life and then as a conquering king who will claim His bride. This majestic vision compels us to live in readiness and joyous expectation, secure in the knowledge that our Bridegroom will indeed return for us.

As we reflect on these truths, let us draw near to our Savior with renewed hearts, embracing the profound spiritual insights that Song of Solomon offers about our relationship with Christ and with one another in the bond of marriage.

Reflective Questions

1. How does understanding the Hebrew wedding customs deepen your appreciation for Christ's sacrifice and promise to return?

2. In what ways does the imagery of Christ as a Bridegroom challenge or enhance your personal faith journey?

3. What role does anticipation play in your spiritual life, and how can you cultivate a more hopeful attitude while waiting for Christ's return?

4. How can the principles of sacrificial love and submission in marriage inspire improvements in other relationships in your life?

5. Reflect on a time when anxiety or insecurity tested your faith. How did you overcome these challenges, and what did you learn about God's character through that experience?

ACTIONABLE STEPS

- **Cultivate Patience and Preparedness:** Foster a spirit of patient anticipation as the Shulamite bride did while waiting for Solomon, focusing on personal spiritual growth and readiness for Christ's return.
- **Equip with Knowledge:** Deepen your understanding of biblical marriage and its symbolism by studying Ephesians 5 and other scriptures that illustrate Christ's relationship with the Church, enhancing your appreciation of divine design.
- **Engage in Reflective Prayer:** Regularly engage in prayer that reflects on the covenant relationship with Christ, similar to the Hebrew betrothal practices, reaffirming your commitment to Him and His teachings.

JOURNALING Prompt

Reflect on the symbolic meanings of the marriage rituals in Song of Solomon. How does this deepen your understanding of Christ's promises to you as part of His bride? Write about your feelings of anticipation for Christ's return and how this shapes your daily life and faith.

LIVING YOUR LOVE STORY OFFICIAL WORKBOOK

MORE THAN MEETS THE EYE

CHAPTER 8
SACRED AND SIZZLING SEX

Let this be your encouragement today: God designed sex not only as a sacred act but as one of the profound joys of marriage, meant to strengthen and celebrate the bond between husband and wife. It is a gift from God, a treasure that should be cherished and protected within the boundaries of marriage. When embraced according to God's plan, it can be a powerful expression of love and unity.

Hebrews 13:4 (NKJV): "Marriage is honorable among all, and the bed undefiled; but fornicators and adulterers God will judge."

In this exploration of Sacred and Sizzling Sex, we delve into the profound depths of what sex means within the sanctity of marriage, as God intended it to be—a powerful, sacred, and joy-filled expression of love between a husband and wife. It is a gift meant to strengthen their bond and express mutual love and commitment. This brings us to our first major point: **the sacredness of sex**. God designed this intimate act not merely as a physical pleasure but as a profound expression of love and commitment within the safety of marriage. This is not just about physicality but about a deep, emotional, and spiritual connection, highlighting the sanctity bestowed upon it by our Creator.

Contrasting sharply with this view is **the perversion of sex by society**. In a world where the lines of biblical morality are increasingly blurred, sex is often misrepresented as mere personal gratification. This misrepresentation leads to damaging behaviors and attitudes that distort this beautiful gift. Recognizing these distortions is crucial as we seek to reclaim and celebrate the truth of sex as a divine expression of love, moving away from the societal view that sees it as a playground for personal pleasure without consequences.

Furthermore, **the impact of cultural degradation on personal and societal health** cannot be ignored. As societal norms drift further from God's design, the consequences become increasingly severe, manifesting in higher rates of addiction, depression, and broken relationships. This understanding prompts us to seek purity and advocate for sexual integrity within our communities, emphasizing the need for a return to the boundaries set by God for our protection and flourishing.

For those who have been hurt or misled about the nature of sexual relationships, **healing and restoration through Christ** offer a beacon of hope. Jesus' healing power is available to restore purity and wholeness, reaffirming that no matter one's past experiences, renewal and joy in this area of life are possible through faith in Him. This promise of restoration is a powerful testament to the transformative power of Christ's love and sacrifice.

Amid the misrepresentations and abuses of sex in our culture, it is vital to remember and teach that **celebrating sex within marriage** is not only permissible but encouraged. Song of Solomon beautifully illustrates the joy and excitement inherent in the marital relationship, providing a stark contrast to the notion that married sex must be dull or perfunctory.

Trust and security form the bedrock of a healthy sexual relationship within marriage. This leads us to understand **the role of trust and security in sexual intimacy**. Just as a bride trusts her groom, establishing a relationship where both partners feel safe and valued is crucial. This sense of security enables both to engage fully and joyfully in their physical relationship, free from fear and full of love.

Reflecting on **sexual intimacy as a reflection of Christ's love for the Church**, we see the ultimate purpose of marriage—to mirror the profound, sacrificial love Christ has for His bride, the Church. This analogy not only elevates the act of marriage above mere physical enjoyment but also embeds it with immense spiritual significance, enhancing our understanding of marital intimacy.

Open communication about desires, expectations, and boundaries is critical in cultivating a fulfilling sexual relationship that honors both spouses and God. Thus, **the importance of communication and mutual respect** in a marriage cannot be overstressed. By fostering an environment where both spouses can speak freely and respectfully about their needs and boundaries, the marital bond is strengthened and enriched.

Many carry scars from past experiences related to sexuality, either through personal choices or the actions of others. **Overcoming past hurts and embracing healing** is essential for experiencing the full joy of sexual intimacy in marriage. Encouraging individuals to seek healing and embrace the renewal offered through Christ is a crucial aspect of Christian counseling and ministry.

Finally, **fostering intimacy through spiritual and emotional connection** is as vital as the physical aspect of marriage. True intimacy involves more than physical connection—it includes emotional closeness and spiritual unity. This deeper connection is cultivated through shared spiritual practices, vulnerabilities, and continuous growth together in Christ.

In our journey through this chapter, we've unpacked the multifaceted aspects of marital intimacy, aiming to restore and celebrate the beautiful, God-given gift of sex within the covenant of marriage. As we continue to reflect on these truths, let us hold fast to the promise that in every aspect of our lives, including our most intimate relationships, we are called to reflect the love, purity, and joy of our relationship with Christ.

Reflective Questions

1. How does understanding the sacredness of sex within marriage change your perspective on its purpose?
2. In what ways has society influenced your views on sexuality, and how can you begin to align those views more closely with biblical standards?
3. What steps can you take to foster better communication about sexual expectations and boundaries within your marriage?
4. How can you support your spouse in healing from past hurts that may be affecting your sexual relationship?
5. What are some practical ways you can build both emotional and spiritual intimacy with your spouse?

Actionable Steps

- **Cultivate** a deeper understanding of the sacredness of sex by studying what the Bible says about it, particularly through books like Song of Solomon and 1 Corinthians.
- **Equip** yourself and your spouse with knowledge and tools for healing by seeking counseling if past sexual wounds are hindering your relationship.
- **Engage** in regular, open conversations with your spouse about your sexual relationship, aiming to deepen trust and understanding.

Journaling Prompt

Reflect on your current views and experiences regarding sexual intimacy. Consider how these align with the biblical perspective of sex as a sacred, joyous, and bonding act within marriage. What steps can you take to move towards a more biblical understanding and expression of sexuality in your marriage?

SACRED AND SIZZLING SEX

LIVING YOUR LOVE STORY OFFICIAL WORKBOOK

CHAPTER 9
WHEN YOU'VE LOST THAT LOVIN' FEELIN'

Chapter 9 When You've Lost That Lovin' Feelin'
"Love is patient, love is kind. It does not envy, it does not boast, it is not proud." – 1 Corinthians 13:4 (NKJV)

"Be kind to one another, tenderhearted, forgiving one another, even as God in Christ forgave you." – Ephesians 4:32 (NKJV)

In **Chapter 9**, "When You've Lost That Lovin' Feelin'," we explore the intricate dance of marriage through the lens of Solomon and the Shulamite, which teaches us that **conflict is inevitable in marriage**. It's a universal truth that no relationship, no matter how steeped in love, is immune to disputes. Understanding this can liberate us from unrealistic expectations and prepare us for healthy **conflict resolution**, which is not only inevitable but also essential for growth and understanding in a marriage.

As we delve into the narrative, we see Solomon's response to a marital spat, which was not marked by coercion or anger but by a symbolic act of leaving myrrh on his wife's door. This act was akin to leaving a bouquet of flowers, a gesture of love and peace rather than assertion of rights. This teaches us the importance of **communicating affection in rejection**. When faced with rejection, responding with a gesture of love can pave the way for healing and reconciliation. It's a poignant reminder that affection, even in the face of disagreement, can be a powerful tool for softening hearts and mending fences.

Furthermore, Solomon's approach underscores a vital lesson about **submission and mutual respect** in relationships. In laying down his rights, he prioritizes his wife's needs over his own, embodying the biblical call for husbands and wives to submit to one another out of reverence for Christ. This mutual submission fosters a deeper respect and understanding between partners, highlighting that the essence of marriage revolves around giving rather than taking.

The story also brings to light the **impact of withholding affection**, both sexually and emotionally. We are reminded that such withholding can lead to temptation and weaken the bonds of marriage. Here, Solomon teaches us that maintaining physical and emotional intimacy is crucial in safeguarding the marital relationship against external and internal pressures.

In the biblical narrative, we also find a profound teaching about the **sexual responsibilities in marriage**. The mutual obligations between spouses to fulfill each other's needs are clear and are intended to prevent the pitfalls of neglect and dissatisfaction. The Scripture advises spouses to not deprive one another, underlining the necessity of attending to each other's desires as a safeguard against temptation.

One of the most striking elements of Solomon's narrative is his refusal to force entry or assert his kingly rights, which teaches us about **Solomon's gentle approach**. His decision to softly engage rather than escalate the conflict speaks volumes about the power of gentleness and self-control in conflict situations. This approach not only de-escalates potential conflicts but also preserves the dignity and respect of both partners.

The **role of prayer in conflict** is another crucial element we draw from this chapter. Turning to prayer in moments of marital strife invites divine guidance and fosters humility and patience. By seeking divine intervention, couples can find the strength to navigate the choppy waters of marital discord with grace and wisdom.

Addressing the **long-term effects of unresolved conflicts**, we learn that letting disputes fester can lead to deep-seated resentment and emotional distance. Therefore, resolving issues promptly and effectively is key to maintaining a healthy, vibrant relationship. Ignoring the small issues today can lead to insurmountable barriers tomorrow.

Lastly, the resolution of conflicts in a marriage is not just about returning to a state of peace but about reinforcing the bond shared by the couple. This narrative emphasizes that **enduring love through submission**—where both partners continually lay down their personal agendas in favor of the relationship's well-being—is essential. This mutual submission, modeled by Solomon, is pivotal for a marriage that not only survives but thrives.

Through these reflections, we see that Solomon and the Shulamite's story is not just an ancient tale but a timeless manual on love, respect, and mutual submission in marriage. Each conflict, rather than being a wedge driving couples apart, can be a bridge bringing them closer, transforming challenges into opportunities for growth and deeper unity.

Reflective Questions

1. How do you typically respond to conflict in your relationship, and what can you learn from Solomon's approach?
2. In what ways can you better communicate affection during times of disagreement with your spouse?
3. How does the concept of mutual submission manifest in your own marriage or relationship?
4. What steps can you take to ensure that conflicts do not lead to long-term damage in your relationship?
5. Reflect on a time when either withholding or receiving affection impacted your relationship. What was learned, and how was the situation resolved?

Actionable Steps

- **Cultivate Understanding**: Make a conscious effort to understand your partner's perspective during conflicts without immediately seeking to be understood.
- **Equip with Tools for Resolution**: Engage in workshops or counseling sessions that focus on conflict resolution to equip both partners with effective communication skills.
- **Engage in Regular Communication**: Set aside time each week to discuss any areas of dissatisfaction in the relationship, ensuring both partners feel heard and valued.

Journaling Prompt

Reflect on the last major conflict you experienced in your relationship. Write about how it was handled and consider how applying Solomon's approach of gentle communication and leaving a symbolic 'bouquet of flowers' might have altered the outcome. What can you do differently in future conflicts to foster peace and understanding?

WHEN YOU'VE LOST THAT LOVIN' FEELIN'

CHAPTER 10

HOW TO GET BACK THAT LOVIN' FEELIN'

"Let all that you do be done with love." – 1 Corinthians 16:14 (NKJV)

"And above all things have fervent love for one another, for 'love will cover a multitude of sins.'" – 1 Peter 4:8 (NKJV)

In exploring **Chapter 10**, "How to Get Back that Lovin' Feelin'," we delve into the complexities and dual nature of love within the context of marriage, discovering that love is both a profound emotion and a deliberate choice. This chapter illustrates the essential truth that while eros, or romantic love, might initially draw us together, it is agape, the sacrificial love modeled by Christ, that sustains relationships over time. By understanding that **love as both emotion and action** is necessary, we learn the practical ways to nurture and sustain our relationships.

Marriage is an ongoing journey of choosing each other day after day, and in this chapter, the emphasis on **the power of choice in love** is paramount. This choice isn't just about staying in love but actively choosing actions that express love, thereby creating an environment where eros can thrive. Actions spurred by agape love often lead to the rekindling of eros, showing us that emotional love can indeed follow from deliberate, loving actions.

To truly **rekindle love through intentional actions**, you might consider revisiting the activities and gestures that initially brought you together. This could be as simple as dedicating time to each other without distractions or returning to the special places that hold significant memories. This approach isn't about waiting for the feelings of love to arise spontaneously but about putting love into motion, thereby allowing the emotions of love to surface naturally.

The foundation of lasting love in any marriage is the selfless, **sacrificial nature of agape love**. This love is not reliant on feelings but is a steadfast choice to act in the best interest of your spouse, even when it's challenging. This chapter stresses that such love ensures the ongoing presence of eros by continuously nurturing the relationship through selflessness and kindness.

When couples face challenges or drift apart, they are often advised to **rediscover the love** they once felt. This isn't just about reminiscing but about actively doing the things that once drew them close. It could be revisiting old love letters, recreating a first date, or simply spending uninterrupted time together. These activities are vital as they serve as reminders of why you fell in love in the first place and can help reignite those feelings.

Navigating through **conflict with love** is another critical point. Conflict, when approached with a spirit of understanding and patience, can actually strengthen a relationship rather than weaken it. This chapter shows that disagreements, when handled with care and respect, can deepen mutual understanding and bring couples closer together.

The **importance of commitment over time** is vividly illustrated through the renewed relationship between Solomon and his bride in the Song of Solomon. Their story is a testament to the power of enduring love that evolves from mere infatuation to a deep, mature connection that spans decades. Their commitment to each other, reflected in continuous loving actions, exemplifies how true love grows and flourishes over time.

Celebrating the victories and the **love rekindled** after overcoming obstacles is just as important as the work it takes to get there. Acknowledging each other's efforts and the journey you've shared reinforces the bond and encourages further growth. Solomon's poetic praises of his wife not only honor her but also reinforce their renewed affection, showing the power of affirmation.

The **spiritual dimensions of love** play a significant role in the strength and resilience of a marriage. By connecting love with spirituality, couples can find a deeper meaning and purpose in their relationship, often leading to a more profound connection that transcends the everyday challenges of life.

Lastly, the journey of love in marriage is one of **continuous learning and adaptation**. As individuals and as a couple, you are always evolving. By committing to learning about each other and adapting to each other's growth, you ensure that your relationship does not stagnate but continues to thrive with each passing year.

Reflective Questions

1. In what ways have you seen **love as both an emotion and a choice** in your own relationship?
2. How can you incorporate more **intentional loving actions** into your daily routine to strengthen your marital bond?

3. Can you recall a time when a **deliberate act of love** helped overcome a challenge in your relationship? What was the outcome?
4. How does your **spiritual belief** influence the way you express love in your marriage?
5. What are some new ways you can **celebrate and acknowledge the love** you have for your partner, especially after overcoming conflicts or challenges?

ACTIONABLE STEPS

- **Cultivate Daily Loving Actions**: Introduce small, daily actions that express love and appreciation for your spouse, such as leaving notes, giving compliments, or engaging in activities your spouse enjoys.
- **Equip with Tools for Spiritual Growth**: Together with your spouse, engage in spiritual activities like prayer, meditation, or study, which can deepen your connection and provide a stronger foundation for your relationship.
- **Engage in Continuous Learning**: Commit to learning something new about your partner regularly, whether through direct conversation, shared experiences, or couple's therapy, to keep the relationship dynamic and evolving.

Journaling Prompt

Reflect on the last time you felt deeply connected with your spouse. What actions or circumstances contributed to this feeling? How can you recreate or foster these conditions more regularly to maintain a strong emotional connection within your marriage?

HOW TO GET BACK THAT LOVIN' FEELIN'

LIVING YOUR LOVE STORY OFFICIAL WORKBOOK

CHAPTER 11
THE GARDENER

In the garden of marriage, you are both the gardener and the guardian. As you tend and nurture the relationship, remember that it grows and flourishes not only through the easy seasons but through every challenge and change. Stay committed, cultivate love diligently, and protect the precious growth that emerges through every season shared together.

"And let us not grow weary while doing good, for in due season we shall reap if we do not lose heart." - Galatians 6:9 (NKJV)

In **Chapter 11: The Gardener**, the deepening of love in marriage unfolds like the growth in a well-tended garden. Over the years, Solomon's admiration for his bride only deepens, shifting from a celebration of her physical beauty to a profound appreciation of her inner qualities. This transition reflects a **mature love that sees beyond the surface**, recognizing and valuing the depths of a partner's soul. It's a vivid reminder that in marriage, as in gardening, the most significant results come from consistent, attentive care over time, not from the fleeting excitement of early moments.

Solomon begins his praise differently in this chapter, starting from the feet and moving upwards, a symbolic gesture showing that **every part of his wife is precious to him**, even those aspects previously overlooked. This perspective is crucial for us today, as it teaches the importance of continuous discovery and appreciation in relationships. It encourages us to always look for new things to cherish in our partners, reinforcing the bond and keeping the relationship dynamic and engaging.

The garden metaphor extends beyond mere admiration, incorporating the spiritual and emotional nurturing each partner in a marriage must provide. **Love is seen as a crop that needs constant tending**—watering, weeding, and fertilizing—to reach its full potential. This chapter underscores the ongoing effort required to maintain a relationship's health and the richness that such effort yields over time.

Conflict and reconciliation are as natural in marriage as storms are to gardens. They can harm or strengthen, depending largely on how they're managed. Solomon's poetic expressions remind us that dealing with issues promptly and lovingly, much like addressing garden pests or diseases quickly, prevents them from causing lasting damage.

Reflecting on **the beauty of seasoned love**, Solomon's words emphasize that true appreciation grows over time, mirroring how the best wines improve with age. This mature love is rich, deep, and abundantly rewarding, offering tastes and experiences that young love cannot. The imagery of a garden in full bloom beautifully encapsulates the flourishing state of a long-nurtured relationship.

Moreover, the chapter highlights the **importance of mutual support and defense** in marriage. Just as Solomon appreciates his wife's strength and loyalty, recognizing her as his protector and supporter, we are reminded that a spouse is not only a lover but also a partner in life's battles.

Respect and trust form the trellis on which the vine of love climbs; without them, it cannot grow. Solomon's tribute to his wife's virtues not only praises her but also reaffirms his commitment and trust in her, essential components for any enduring relationship.

Finally, this chapter serves as an **encouragement to all married couples** to continue investing in their relationships. Like a gardener who patiently tends to his plants, knowing that the harvest is still months away, we must nurture our relationships with the same faith and patience.

Reflective Questions

1. How can you start seeing and appreciating the less obvious qualities in your spouse?
2. What daily nurturing does your relationship need to keep it healthy and growing?
3. How do you handle conflicts? Does it strengthen your relationship, or does it leave scars?
4. In what ways can you celebrate the mature beauty of your relationship today?
5. How can trust and mutual support be further developed in your relationship?

Actionable Steps

- **Cultivate Daily Appreciation:** Make it a daily practice to compliment or express appreciation for

your spouse, focusing on different qualities each time.
- **Equip with Communication Tools:** Regularly set time aside to discuss your relationship openly and honestly, aiming to strengthen your communication and understanding.
- **Engage in Mutual Activities:** Find activities that both of you enjoy or have wanted to try, and commit to doing them together, strengthening your bond through shared experiences.

JOURNALING **Prompt**

Reflect on your relationship as if it were a garden. What parts are flourishing, and what parts need more attention? How can you tend to these neglected areas to ensure the entire garden thrives?

THE GARDENER

LIVING YOUR LOVE STORY OFFICIAL WORKBOOK

CHAPTER 12
LOVING YOUR SECOND LIKE YOUR FIRST

Endure in love as it matures, finding new depths and joys even as years pass. God's intention for marriage is to see it thrive through every season of life, grounded in devotion and mutual respect.

"Set me as a seal upon your heart, as a seal upon your arm; for love is as strong as death, jealousy as cruel as the grave; its flames are flames of fire, a most vehement flame." (Song of Solomon 8:6, NKJV)

As we explore **Chapter 12: Loving Your Second Like Your First**, we delve into the heart of enduring love, a journey through the lifecycle of a relationship that reflects both divine orchestration and human commitment. This chapter isn't merely a continuation of a love story; it is a reaffirmation of the timeless truth that committed relationships can and should flourish over time.

When considering the evolution of love in a long-term partnership, we recognize that **committed love is pleasurable**. It's a common misconception that long-term relationships are destined to lose their sparkle and become mundane. However, the true essence of mature love is its ability to grow richer and more delightful with each passing year. As the couple in Song of Solomon demonstrates, their later years are not marked by boredom but by a renewed zest for companionship, where even a simple walk together is an opportunity for romance and deeper connection.

This brings us to the realization that **committed love is providential**. In the grand design of our lives, our relationships are not merely happenstances but are woven into the larger tapestry of our destinies. Recognizing that our significant others have been placed in our lives for a reason can transform the way we cherish and nurture our relationships. It invites a perspective of gratitude and purpose, encouraging us to view every challenge and joy as part of a greater plan.

Another profound insight from this chapter is that **committed love is permanent**. Love, in its truest form, is not transient but enduring. The analogy of love being as strong as death, where its bond is unbreakable and its essence unquenchable, serves to remind us of the depth and permanence of true love. It's a force that withstands trials and time, growing only stronger in the face of life's tempests.

Moreover, the chapter beautifully illustrates that **committed love is pure**. As the narrative of the Shulamite and her transition from a protected young woman to a loving wife unfolds, we see the beauty of a love that reserves itself solely for one's partner. This exclusivity is the cornerstone of trust and commitment in a relationship, where both partners feel secure and valued in their unique bond.

Finally, we learn that **committed love remembers the past**. Recounting the origins of a relationship can be a powerful way to keep the flame of love alive. Remembering how you met, the early challenges you overcame together, and the growth you've experienced can reignite passion and appreciation for each other. It serves as a reminder that every day spent together is a building block in the edifice of a lifelong love.

REFLECTIVE QUESTIONS

1. How have you seen your love evolve from the early days of your relationship to now?
2. In what ways can you see God's providence at work in your relationship?
3. What practices have you implemented to ensure your love remains permanent and unyielding to life's challenges?
4. How do you maintain purity in your relationship, ensuring it remains reserved and special just for your spouse?
5. How often do you reminisce about your early days together, and how does this strengthen your bond?

ACTIONABLE STEPS

- **Cultivate**: Dedicate time each week to reflect on the journey you've shared with your spouse, acknowledging how each phase of your relationship has contributed to your growth as a couple.
- **Equip**: Set up regular 'relationship audits' where you openly discuss areas of strength and improvement in your relationship, ensuring both partners feel heard and valued.

- **Engage:** Create new traditions or revisit old ones that have special meaning to both of you, as a way to keep the history and romance alive in your relationship.

Journaling Prompt

Reflect on a moment in your relationship that felt pivotal or defining. Describe how this moment has shaped the way you view your partner and the overall trajectory of your relationship. How does remembering this moment influence your feelings towards your spouse today?

LOVING YOUR SECOND LIKE YOUR FIRST

LIVING YOUR LOVE STORY OFFICIAL WORKBOOK

ABOUT THE PUBLISHER

D DESTINY IMAGE

Destiny Image is a prophetic Christian publisher dedicated to empowering believers through Spirit-led messages. Our mission is to equip and inspire individuals to fulfill their God-given destinies by providing transformative resources that resonate with the Charismatic and Pentecostal faith.

We specialize in books, blogs, and back cover copies that reflect prophetic insights, dynamic teachings, and testimonies of faith. Our commitment to fostering spiritual growth and kingdom impact makes Destiny Image a beacon for those seeking to deepen their relationship with God and embrace their calling in the power of the Holy Spirit.